The Raz/Shumaker Prairie Schooner Book Prize in Poetry

Editor Kwame Dawes

MIGHT KINDRED

Mónica Gomery

University of Nebraska Press   Lincoln

Acknowledgments for the use of previously
published material appear on pages 77–78, which
constitute an extension of the copyright page.

The University of Nebraska Press is part of a land-
grant institution with campuses and programs on the
past, present, and future homelands of the Pawnee,
Ponca, Otoe-Missouria, Omaha, Dakota, Lakota, Kaw,
Cheyenne, and Arapaho Peoples, as well as those of the
relocated Ho-Chunk, Sac and Fox, and Iowa Peoples.

Library of Congress Cataloging-in-Publication Data
Names: Gomery, Mónica, author.
Title: Might kindred / Mónica Gomery.
Description: Lincoln: University of Nebraska
Press, [2022] | Series: The Raz/Shumaker
prairie schooner book prize in poetry
Identifiers: LCCN 2022002093
ISBN 9781496232397 (paperback)
ISBN 9781496233851 (epub)
ISBN 9781496233868 (pdf)
Subjects: BISAC: POETRY / American /
General | LCGFT: Poetry.
Classification: LCC PS3607.O48755 M54 2022 |
DDC 811/.6—dc23/eng/20220308
LC record available at https://lccn.loc.gov/2022002093

Designed and set in Garamond Premier Pro by L. Auten.

Contents

Self-Portrait with
Airplane Turbulence   1

Theology   2

Emblanquecer   3

Immigrant Elegy for Ávila   4

Family Is an Illumination
of Shoulders   5

Ghazal for a First Lover   6

Might Kindred   7

Prologue   9

When My Sister Visits   13

Here   14

God Queers the Mountain   15

It Isn't Easy to Speak   16

Falling Out   18

A Poem with Two
Memories of Venezuela   20

Letter to Myself from
My Great Grandmother   22

Origin Stories   23

Abecedario   24

When My Sister Visits   27

After Pulse   28

The Synagogue Membership
Assembles to Discuss the
Fascist Presidency   30

Imaginative Exercise in
the Study of Epigenetics   32

Dendrochronology of Hair   34

Ode to the Poop Bag   36

The Oldest Form of Prayer   38

Now We Live Together   40

Because It Is Elul   42

When My Sister Visits   47

We Thanked Her by
Digging a Hole   48

Fragments of an Anthem   50

Banishing Loneliness   52

Here   54

A Poem About a Book
About Venezuela   56

Sleeping in Hurricane
Season   59

Emblanquecer   61

Ghazal for a Year   62

Halleluyah   63

We Walked Dahlias
to Her Front Porch   67

I Thought I Was Done
Writing About My Dead   68

Ghazal for God &
Wellbutrin   70

The Poet Considers If
Her Body Belongs to Her   71

When My Sister Visits   73

Here   74

Love Letter   75

Acknowledgments   77

Notes   81

MIGHT KINDRED

the future is already full;
it is much older and larger than our present;
and we are the aliens in it.

—Ursula K. Le Guin

Most days, I stand at the edge of the continent
and shout our glitterest names in my ugliest language.

—Franny Choi

SELF-PORTRAIT WITH AIRPLANE TURBULENCE

I don't know what I am, but I am not
one incarnation. 7 miles over the city
the plane bucks between tar-coated angels

and night's groaning light bulbs.
On my way home from una visita:
my grandmother, 100 years packed
into her, coral and mammal.

She pressed my hand
in hers, said *esta manita tan suave.*
My body obeys, begins tumble,

breath caught between gullet
and fingers switching the music:
soundtrack I could die to, some way

to give thanks. Scorpio moon,
eyes wheel up, my abuela already cupping
my face in her palms, coos bendiciones.

I have washed the dead before. I know
exactly how many buckets of water.

THEOLOGY

Baby, I went to seminary for theology.

They taught me every Thou is a funnel for the big bright You.
They taught me God's erotics would come to me in dreams.

Put your queer shoulder to the wheel, they said, and *push
your palm into the center of the earth*; love dissolves us
into people without timepieces or apology.

Sometimes I speak to our unhad child.

She will not be conceived biblically;
she will however be named Selah!
and her many parents will be fluent in the lute.

Say *Hoshana* and it slams at my heart
like a great gust of God's wind.

I asked the baby and she said *gender*, *rhizomes*,
sieve, *shoulder blades*, and *apa*, her mouth says *salt*,
her hands like starfish gripping for ghosts.

We took a paintbrush and put these words up
on the doorframe above her crib:

I have a parent whose parental name is spoken as my Hungarian great grandfather's
parental name, their breasts will be my body's first several hundred cups of water.

Our fathers and their fathers' fathers' fathers' fathers' fathers could not
imagine us, but at least two of them were queer, glowed queerly in the dark.

EMBLANQUECER

When I was born, the air was pale and green and gold.
They came to the United States to be a bigger highway.
They came to Venezuela when Perez Jimenez decided
to *emblanquecer la raza*. What this country doesn't know
could be another country altogether. *Emblanquecer*
looks like *embalm* to me. How lifeless things become
enshrined, instead of being turned back into earth
when they stop sourcing life. When I was born, my oxygen
was pressurized, a cabin in an aircraft hovering no homelands.
My brother making shadow puppets against corrugated walls.
And then more siblings came and with them the unsiblings.
At stake: the always airplane upping me away from. Small
islands are affixed to me. The other white kids call them *freckles*;
the cousins say *lunares*. *Lunar* like my other mother calendar.
Continents float by like elephants. Whiteness smooth and supple
on the mouths and mortgages of my relations. It's very hard
to be something by way of boat or trunk. By way of asthmatic
empire. Or maybe all the time I spend negating what I am
is just avoidance. At stake: so many lives, so many murderous
relations. Compelled by smell, butterflies migrate toward
milkweed miles away, compelled by smell's white compass.
Every time I try to write this down, the words start to dart
away from me. It is a bandaged half-dream, a bungled
nightmare. *This is someone else's map*, I think, pointing wildly
in the dark. No one is here but me. And all my ghosts.
I pull the documents like eyelids over me. Citizenship
papers. Repatriation. I pull the curtains up.

If you take a child to the mountain
do not expect the mountain to not live inside the child.
Do not expect that something mountainous will not rise
inside the child, yielding light and shadow. If you drive
a child through a valley, through highway cut between
the majesty of mountain—have you ever seen a child
at the window of a car? If you put a child
in the back seat of a cab that lifts along the valley
for an hour, do not expect those small wet marble eyes
not to gape and peer and gather up the mountain.
If you nestle a child against the contour of the mountain
every winter of her bony bright-skinned life, chasing
turtles in the backyard of a house, watch
the turtle bump the avocado tree then release
a grassing whisper, watch the child learn
to listen, air staccato-thick with sapos popping
warm but shrill and blooming into night.
If you bring a child up alongside mountain
in a valley so lush it makes the child
dizzy, hairs springing from her legs, her arms,
to imitate the tropic density, if you put a mountain
in a child's mouth, her tongue will form a shape around it
like a fierce and sighing river, like a road between the city
and the sea. To a child, what's the difference
between mountain, mother, highway, river?
Between coastline, cousin, anger, longing?
Which language did you teach her, Spanish, Mountain, English?
We'll call it mountain syndrome, slight unbelonging looming
taller inside a child than might be known, and rising up behind
her shoulders telling stories about soil, streambeds,
confessing something in a mountain language, confessing
something in a language better fit for flash floods.
Forests raining language through their constant canopies.

FAMILY IS AN ILLUMINATION OF SHOULDERS

Walking the ocean with my mother, she's every age
she's ever been. My shoulder cupped in the shadow
of her shoulder, nested against the heaving shoulders

of the sea. All of us breathing, all of us threaded by salt.
My lover and I decide to parent a dog. Continent
of paddling fur, clawed toe on my knee, hospitality

of eyes that say *more*. We used to be two shoulders
brushing, now *more*. Love smells of earth, dander,
and rain. At night I write letters to my grandmother's

brother. *Dear Mendi*, my thoughts become fingers,
yellowed hands one hundred years old. *Mendi
of the boats*, needle threading island to island,

I know you, my eyebrows grow closer together
on the wet bridge between bedroom and cousin,
Mendi of the boats that left Europe. My lover and I visit

my grandmother, sit elbows touching as she asks
about Russia in Spanish. Asks them, *cuantos idiomas?*
Asks us, *how many beds do you sleep in?* We don't lie

and we don't tell the truth, we just give her our eyes.
Don't tell her, my mother reminds me every visit.
Mendi of the traveling forearms, Mendi of sand, long buried

north of Jerusalem. *Mendi have you seen, in these countries
the cities are too far away from the sea, granddaughters an ocean
apart from their mothers, of course they would wind up in bed*

with more breasts. Surely a creature with no language
can more easily love me. A skull mossed over with
black and white spots, ducking into my crotch

as an act of affection. Beside a small lapping beast,
I know I am a beast, hot curve of her belly leaning
into my thigh. I push my face into her face.

GHAZAL FOR A FIRST LOVER

When I first took her or she took me, sanded
and bagged me, loosened up my eyes

Sun was our planet, broken into arrows, heat along
our arms, burned, burnt, dissolving into *ay's*

Mouthed weather, marsh of sheets, splintered skin
where now she buried salt, my gorgeous demise

I tried not to name what came for me, yet: elbow, kneecap,
chin hair, waves of smell grafted to cupping hands, overflowing eyes

Grew me longer than the length of me, myself gone reaching,
reaping—how, silly me, I thought I'd ever used before my eyes.

MIGHT KINDRED

Sitting next to a queer poet
at the reading my shoulder

houses a tiny rose bud
its petals wound tightly

against its other petals. Is this
a queer poetics the way my

body becomes terrarium
at the chance of recognition?

At the front in the dark
of the room a poet builds

the city with his teeth and I
become the smallest petal

on the smallest flower
in the wildest field of words

God of desire who rules
that quiet sky, friendship

bring me a cousin a cousin a cousin
bring me a soft plot of soil

Meet me in the space between
native countries, city wildflower-lush

where blue becomes blue. I want
to tell you a story thick

with maroons. Praise how we tip
toward, spill bright petals, praise glass

opening out—*is this*
queer poetics? God of fragile

new friendship, war
of tender on asphalt

in front of this stranger
I unhook, small surgery

offered in case we might
kindness, might ardor

together *Meet me queer
in the city*, might kindred

might light a match

I have longed for
a fire of flowers.

I went down to the river, the light made plaid with trees. I knelt beside the river, felt its broiling motion. The sky a net.

I saw him there. My ancestor. Curious with bones, long limbed. He stepped out from behind a tree. He looked at me with undemanding eyes. Upturned his palms.

The river churned and babbled. Chortled. Gushed. The river sang its swelling song, its onward song, its carrying the weather song. The river carried anything I gave it, and so I gave some things.

I did not give it folded bits of paper. Instead I gave the river muddy blue, that blue that lives inside me. Wetness cupped between the bulbs of my two shoulders.

I leaned forward, poured out blue, and gave it to the river.

So often too afraid to become an out-loud living person in this century. Blue pouring out.

The confusion I have felt; the trades my people made for safety; someone else's grief. Blue sifting into blue.

I gathered all that murky water, its silt and darkened turquoise swirling. I tipped it toward the river, poured it in as best I could.

The river shimmered back at me, it ate my fear and shame. The sky alive inside the river. The stones clapped and rocked against the water.

My ancestor, long oval face and broomstick fingers, watched. Not with a smile and not without a smile.

The river ate my water and rushed its ruffled skirts downstream. The river silk and mesh and tulle and linen, water weaving as it ate my water, careened my water, and kept on rivering away from me.

I didn't know if time was moving forward or backward along the river's trail. I didn't know if the water I gave it traveled toward the future or the past.

I looked at my ancestor who looked at me. I looked at the purpling sky. I looked at my knees, browned against the river's edge. I knew somewhere the river would meet the sea, blue becoming salt becoming bluer.

I waited for something to speak my name. And because everything around me was my name, it did.

WHEN MY SISTER VISITS

she likes to smoke, much like my brother.
She rolls her own, dense with flora
still growing, and a vaporous air fills
the room. Saplings crop up between
bookshelves, a swamp sprouts waxy grasses
over the sink. I keep trying to tell her I don't
have a sister. She suggests that we arm wrestle.
When I say that's not how I was raised
she tilts her head and says nothing. Or she
strokes my hair and says nothing.

The week after a shooting in your neighborhood, you walk past the bunches of flowers packed onto the doorstep in their pastoral colors, with autumn hinged upon the signposts and every entryway. A bullet hole announces itself in the front window of your storefront office and another memorial leaps off the curb with its watercolor prayers, *Let there be light, Oh God let the violence end*, and more flowers. You turn your shoulder into the unlocking door and stand before a library of names, what some would call innocent and some would call guilty, arranged by their last name their street name their first name their first kiss the name of their third and fourth kiss their uncle the name of the park beside the first house they lived in the third house they lived in. The woman who runs the dry cleaning and shoe repair down the street looks into your eyes with her trumpeting kindness, says, *It doesn't matter good neighborhood, bad*, you're thinking innocent guilty good neighbor bad neighbor, what's the score when the flowers give off this glow, and the haze of the day comes down on a curtain of sadness, and a neighborhood stutters its news corner to corner. A woman is dead and a boy is hospitalized, and a car leapt down the street its tires spinning spirals of sadness. Now the votive candles flicker their hazed halleluyah on the sidewalk, the trees turning gold, a beckoning gold. The alderman has called a meeting on the corner and all day people pause at the storefront window of your office and look into the bullet hole, they look around the bullet hole, one sticks their finger through it. No one has picked up the broken glass and some of them have clipboards. All day they shuffle their feet by the window, run their hands over the soft wilt of the flowers in pinks and in the saddest shade of green you've seen this week. At the end of the workday the camera crew comes back as the sky comes down gold off its hinges. The alderman uses the word *loitering* to deliver a violence against the people who've lived here for many years longer than you have. Some of them have lived here fifty times as long, have planted and tended gardens of blue sage, glowing lament, and laughing thick-tongued orange tulips, clustered onto curbs and corners and autumns bundled into autumns. *Let there be light*, whispers the watercolor memorial and the flickering candle. Someone laid it flush with the sidewalk so that you have to look down as you pass the bullet hole, pass by the pancake shop, looking for something that lives close to the ground.

The last time I taught the story about the mountain, I tented my fingers into a mountain. *See what I did there?* and people laughed, then leaned closer, to consider the base of the mountain, thumb touching thumb, or to consider the peak where my fingers rested triangularly together. In the story, God raises the mountain over the people, either lifting it to hover or flipping it by inverting the triangle, plunging the heavenly peak toward the earth.

To be a human being is to walk that bridge slung between what is mortal and what is sky.

We call that story "Mountain Like Cask" or "Mountain Like Rooftop" or "The Threat of the Law." But I'm thinking let's call it *God Queers the Mountain*. Master of Inversions, insisting the world is capable of being in ways we never saw coming.

One student says, *If God flipped the mountain, then something is falling off of the mountain toward the people.* This had never occurred to me, and now I imagine the landslide of rocks, branches, and scripture, pouring down the face of the upside-down mountain at the people who stand there and tremble, try to keep their palms open.

To be a human being is to encounter debris.

To be human is to keep breathing as the gifts and the threats of the mountain hurl toward you.

At the reading, the trans novelist talks about rewriting Norse and Greek myths. Someone asks, *What is it about the mythic and fabulist that so populates the queer imagination?* Someone else responds, *Archetypes, belonging, new roots.* Later that night a friend asks me, *Why did it feel like it mattered so much when you made the mountain with your hands?*

We are slung to the mountain. When it flips we flip, when it trembles we tremble. When it takes a new body, when it transforms its shape. When it is lonely, or stable, or wise.

To be queer means to listen for the stories of ancestors and find yourself stacked up against trees, boulders, breathing the breath of the mountain, the inverted mountain.

IT ISN'T EASY TO SPEAK

but light does embrace
us from the side.

Shadows long for us.
Hair still grows. It isn't
easy to heal but generosity
can scale a wall.

I hold people together
in my bare hands,
crowding them in,
promising them a location
tucked against grooves
in my fingers. I hurt them
with the holding. I hurt them
but also sometimes
it works.

It is frantic, loving people
between your fingers.
Tucking them in.

Some days I am brute.
I snap flowers from
inexperienced necks
with my thumbs, I wear
all my shirts backward.

Some days I am crammed
between my own teeth.

The world coughs.
The world lifts her skirt.
We can't tell whether
we are her concern.

After I sing to you
my eyelashes will fall
into the soup, my
skin will unripen.

Someone once
explained to me
that guilt is a fact
and shame is a wound.
That love is not
the opposite of harm.

People come down
over me, people
precipitate.
I open my hands
to catch, not them,
but their falling.

FALLING OUT

When we were young in another life all snarling
our hair. We: a private language. We ate

each other's hands. Us a danger that we
shared. I've hard-loved you leaning

into you with all my weight, loved like a teething
moon till teeth came cracking down, showering

my ankles. I loved/you pushed/small cage
built out of it. The word I kept was *patient*.

The smell of earth-dragged oak. Air holding
our long particles. We piled thing on top of thing,

fingers touching under sand. Hands togethering,
we built, but couldn't salivate. I had your left

knee, maybe eyelash as my own.
Apparently I can grow wings. Sometimes

the letting go is slow and sudden, both.
After years of wrangling love's shadow

to the ground, we realize our hands
are empty, bodies bruised but floating, Water

Water, Oh you've drowned me, scoured me.
Now I am clean. The love I once wore heavy

now sails, unaffixed to me. I've longed
so hard it snapped my body

into halves. So hard I turned
through myself like wind washing a veil.

All these years I thought that I was
loving you, but I was mourning you

and now it's done. I lay down the work, step
to the left. I look at it there.

It takes a breath.
Then, I take a breath.

A POEM WITH TWO MEMORIES OF VENEZUELA

The first time her hair was sunlight and it moved in loud wet rivulets, and it warmed me, and it darkened my eyebrows to be so close to her. She passed small beads of fruit into my mouth. My teeth became seeds and my blood became guava. My own hair became highways, knotted and tangled, and she patted my exhaust-fuming head to tell me I was beautiful. I was a child, squinting into how huge and how warm and how mine and not mine her body. The plane ride home was always about something unhitching and floating away. A sterilizing, dream-bleary goodbye. Arriving home with one less limb or finger, buttons wiggled loose on their threads, tongue slack on jangling teeth.

Later, when I became too busy for her, lines of age scored both our cheeks and skin spattered from the cloud-lust of storms. From great distances I spoke her name aloud, then less, then more, her gales up-throating a continent, scaling a continent like a stairwell to sweep a voice through the wind chime of my memory. She carved me out of distance, condensation, certain objects stowed in the closet in the room my grandmother would stay in when she'd come to visit. She carved me out of oil-slick waters, salt-encrusted rains, mud cascading over city hills becoming clay, carrying dust of human origins. She carved me out of pixelated images of street protests, socialist revolutions, grocery stores with barren shelves. She slid a tongue into my mouth, so I've made do with two. She taught me supple light, and forests lacing between coasts, and pregnant mammals braying on their haunches in the always-summer wind.

It's hard to say what an immigrant is. A cluster of ants held in the palm. See how they circulate urgent on skin, see how they spiral, how their legs never stop moving. Certain children are prone to tip over the rock and upturn a whole city of ants, then track their escape routes.

It's hard to say what an immigrant is. There is a place in you, fertile as soil but changeling as weather. There's a place in you. It raised you and gave you the letters of too many languages, it gave you your tenderness, your distance, your rage.

What a child of an immigrant is. Thrice born, three sets of eyes. Belonging to no one. Carrying documents written with invisible ink. Speaking languages scavenged from cousins and radio hosts. Or else speaking the silence, that primary language of people who have been exactly everywhere and nowhere, excavated and learned by the gaps in between.

LETTER TO MYSELF FROM MY GREAT GRANDMOTHER

Remember, when they took our portrait
they had not invented smiling for the camera.

Do not think we were other than stones
in boiling water, clapping together, making that steam.

Girl with mercury coursing your bird-bones.
Did you think it was you who invented this brittle

strength? Girl in the clothing of children and men.
Girl who cannot stop reading.

I laid the seed of you into a bed of cabbage.
Did you think we have not glowed in the dark

somewhere before? I chased the demons
through the night rooms of the house.

When I caught them they started to pull branches
in for the funeral pyre. I told them your name.

They grew quiet, said nothing. Your peculiar
name, burning a charm through my tongue.

Girl with dozens of tiny hairs that light up
when you're afraid. I loved women and the pearls

of their friendship. Wouldn't you like to know how.
Wouldn't you like to know how I preferred

my potatoes. Wouldn't you like to taste now
the salt of the soil that gave you my body.

Girl, grow your nails, stop stripping them back
with your teeth. You'll need your sharpest

bones for a demon more serious
than your own doubt.

In my dreams I drank something other
than water and now you are drunk.

ORIGIN STORIES

If you don't ask
the poet if anyone
in her family
was a poet,
you will miss
the story of
her grandmother
who wrote long-form
poems advertising
groceries in Santiago,
and you will miss
the story about
her other
grandmother
who sang
for the radio,
composed
her own
lyrics.

Why wouldn't
you assume
she's got poets
in her family.

When women talk
the air is sliced
like skins of fish.

When women talk
creation bends
its knees.

ABECEDARIO

abuela idioma whiteness winter
buzón pasaporte laundered lettered
country nowhere kitchen stranger

doña valle playa kitchen
ocean edges mountain mountain
forest pueblo paper fringes

fathers scissors step-aunts soldiers
husband airport stranger pulling
husband kuchen kitchen sugar

kitchen stranger airport kitchen
kuchen knuckles scissors nowhere
mezcla mapa sala masa

mountain kitchen stitching tongue
pulling passport seafloor lengua
pine trees prayer pregunta portal

prayerbook pine trees candles matches
silence selva sinagoga
suitcase scissors stranger lengua

sisters step-aunts brother soldiers

soldiers soldiers soldiers soldiers
soldiers soldiers soldiers soldiers
soldiers soldiers soldiers soldiers

velas matches fuego flame
whiteness stitching silence mundo
soldiers silence stitching soldiers

pueblo mapa playa mundo
mountain passport mongrel mundo
soldiers ocean stranger mundo

茭

WHEN MY SISTER VISITS

she talks about people we know but
they all have some other name:
Wind Wheel Turning, Dark as Earth, Song
on Infinite Loop. She keeps trying on my jackets.
I keep asking her if she has met my brother.
I keep asking if she has seen my cousin, on his way
to Mexico City from Caracas with his girlfriend
searching for work. She says, *I rode the bus here
with your cousin at the wheel.*

AFTER PULSE

*—in memory of the victims of the Pulse nightclub shooting,
Orlando, June 2016*

Here is the quietest place.

The crease at the fold of the body, that place that you tuck yourself into when you are afraid, when the storms shake the world and the rains come in bullets and there is a roof blocking the sky and the roof makes things less safe, when enclosures imprison, when darkness was freedom and becomes, suddenly, death.

Here is the silence, how it draws you toward it by calling the names of every one of your wounds. Not just the headlines but each intimate name, named by its shadow and the names of how many that run in a blood-let alongside the walkway, where blood was a river dried over and rising again.

We say, *Say their names*, and we *say* and we *say*, and the litany wrestles our tongues from our mouths.

At the vigil he told us, *Each of these names is a verse of Quran. Each of the fallen was a sign of God in the world.* At the vigil our hands have grown candles in place of our fingers. Wicks ignite ten flames of remembrance on each of our bodies, and we lift our hands toward the roof, all flamey and burning, because who decided anyway that this vigil should take place inside?

Up go the hands, and up climb the flames, and as we are mourning we are burning it down.

We are burning it down. Let's try again once the fire's done eating. Let's build from the heart.

Here is cavernous grief. Its walls echo with hollow. Its name: Can't Hold On. The cavern is an optical illusion, it wants you to think you are alone inside its sticky wet walls. It wants you to tremble here, no language for loss. No compass for rage, no context for mess.

Don't be mess, don't be dizzy, the grief goads and cajoles. *Don't be a wrecked ship in the night, wracked up against the walls of a fortress, wood splintered apart and passengers missing. Don't be a ship on its way between countries, or a raft, or a raft filled with children and parents needing somewhere to land. Don't be between borders, don't be* for *other people. Do not be* for *one another*—the cavernous grief echoes, its voice harsh as it bounces against its own walls.

Here is blood, *don't drink it, don't touch it, or look directly at it*, even though it is as red as your own or still redder. Blue on the inside, red on the outside, and glinting with sequins both inside and outside. Here the blood throbs your mouth, gathers at the shoreline of lips, the islands of teeth, the blood swells the coast of you, rises in tide. Blood—is it yours? Is it someone's little brother's? Prying apart lips, blood in the gums, blood emerging as names like calligraphied ribbons on satin in red. *Say their names*, bleed for this, blood-let the wound of the mouth.

And it comes forth as the quiet, because it is grief. Beyond words but contains words, because it is candlelight, because it is kaddish, because it is scripture and speechlessness speaking.

Burn it down, says the blood, says the worn sacrament. *Put your candle hand into the palm of another's and another's, and don't fear the fire, it will gather in heat and in force and you'll be connected, we will all be connected, let it burn to the ground and when it is over the earth will know what to do next.*

THE SYNAGOGUE MEMBERSHIP ASSEMBLES
TO DISCUSS THE FASCIST PRESIDENCY

Room lit with the static of stacked generations.
Everyone leaning out of their chairs toward
everyone else leaning out of their chairs.

Music above and below us like water.

What are we?
and someone says *cycle*,
someone says *orbit*, *marionettes*.

Bodies like seagrass hustle and surge
against tide and nation, longing
for a luminous wildgrass
that could weave us a home.
But, look: we have shoulders
so we know we exist.

America menaces its new and old face.
We are Chinese American, Arkansas Black,
Austro Hungarian, Long Island Italian,
Egyptian, Korean. All of us Jews. Our diaspora
teeters on its old and old again edge.

Our resident linguist explains:
*"Jew" is the only one-syllable name
for a people. This is part of the violence.*
Next to him someone tilts their head
and says *Sikh*, but the theory prevails
in the room. Dozens of bodies
re-metabolize something spat,
something said to mean *filth*.

Bodies gathering up their own bones
and their water, holding them close,

which takes effort on this city block
in America. *I want us to belong to each
other but not because our president hates us.*
Eyelashes slip along spines of books,
riotous soil beneath carpet, a churning.

What are we—out there, or to one another?
Are we a basket, wildflowers and garlic,
a stairwell, lost coin, a gun barrel jammed
or unjammed by bright summer petals?
Whose hands, whose story of hands
do we belong to, and can a people
belong to a dreaming machine?

Room lit with tongues tacked up
in new and old shapes, song
a canopy opening over our heads,
seafloor of song under floor
beneath soil and bones.

*What if music can't answer
these kinds of questions?*

These questions, jammed
in the sentences our grandparents
spoke, in the pause between exhale
and molar, mouths soundless with asking,
and inside us an unquenchable yearning
to build a boat.

IMAGINATIVE EXERCISE IN THE STUDY OF EPIGENETICS

Remember the body and its brave hankerings.

I pillow down a fortress, find you there. I rock and hum with old-growth forests. I strange peppers and salts. I wanted to believe in somewhere else—a world alongside this one, tucked and warriored. A place for people like us—feathers flung high waists belting birdsongs—where we could catch each other, dig a trench and lay together, dusted in by our own beauty, pealing wonder down and carrying our scarloads and mirrorlaughing in each other's face. Tendergentled, gendercracked and grain for grain of hidden photographs, deserts, mountains buried under mountains, rivers thralling rivers, rushing over, tumbledown my bravest loves, my keeping ones, my candlelit, my kept.

Swarming us with us until we are safe enough. Our tallness, our internal tallness, the clean abrasive edges of our eyes taken by night's blue-belted hammering. Taken by wide-hearted lusting after the lost siblings. I wanted to construct a world for us. To join the architects of our already future, lay world down alongside world, the process of remembering a somewhere else where a part of us is already residing. Somewhere lit by starlight, somewhere scrawled by skin and breath.

Remember the body and its cousins.

Streams and hilltops, sand dunes and sea. Remember forests, peninsular coastlines, deserts, remember a lake. One lake, one stone in the palm of a hand, one arc between thrown and sunk, one sky vaulting over a family of relations. Remember knotting the bandana around your neck and sloping through the green-eyed tree-lined path, searching for the voices. Remember what the trees sound like when they talk to you, the way their silence enters you, not as silence but as guidance.

Imagine there's a way not to pass along the barbs and sharps. How a body might contour through a day without cringed choreography. Picture a you that barely resembles you. Your unshamed descendants, motored by something other than hot elbows, humiliated knees, sore cheeks. Motored by something other than panic and scorch as they curve and propel. What their laugh sounds like. What their faces do when they pray. What limbs they have, how trusting and how proud their limbs.

DENDROCHRONOLOGY OF HAIR

Slung up onto the instrument. All those years
you thought it was "wavy." Wet whorl

of Caribbean and tongue of crazed sunlight.
Green sigh of New England fingering through.

A waltz of Romania, hilltop Slovak breeze,
praise-songs of your people twisting and twisting.

All those years you thought it deserved to be
pressed against the hot blade. Motion is scratched

through your crowded wind map. Chime of light,
leg of insect, cutting and cutting. Time capsule

of mother. Nail clipping of grandmother.
Her hands wrung up on the machine,

her lungs telling the story of war.
Breath belaboring breath becomes bead

of transmission, from her mouth you are bloomed
and from her spittle your hair. Passport of: chopped.

Passport of: grieving. Reverb of blow-dry. Echo and echo
of having been child. The '90s pour through. The feathers

don't stick. All those years you thought thickness
was its own language foreboding. All those years

you pinned blonde girls to the altar, drenching in itch.
The sound of a comb being scratched against longing.

Wild discoveries, spirals and zephyrs. The grid falls away.
The labyrinth announces her reign. Passport of: dignity.

Passport of: strange. And twinkling against
summer night. Razors past twenty. Some forests within you

grow deeper while others fall ashen. Suddenly scalp
is a belonging. Passport of: see me. Passport of: Queer.

The sound of a butter knife gliding through salt crystals.
Hands against crown become palm prints of loving.

Friendship a language spoken by scissors. Passport of: fur.
Passport of: mammal. Oil aquifers slicking and slicking

with beauty. Rain is accomplice. Ocean becomes angel.
Your dead start referring to you with the nickname

of *longneck*, the only place you are tall. The wind
of the shore of the sea slaps against you

bare skinned on the bridge between thinking
and knowing, your mane peeking over the cliff

of your forehead, getting alive,
getting and getting alive.

ODE TO THE POOP BAG

If there wasn't a clear way to scrapheap
the odor and texture of shit, I don't know
that this tongueful of sweetness could have
survived. Imagine every day's hours swallowed
by excrement, nowhere to step, every shoe
slathered in chaos and stank. So thank you
degradable plastic, thank you durable casing,
tunnel of hygiene that slips over the small stockpile
announcing itself on the grass. Thank you gloved
hand unchaste, thank you luggage for dung,
thank you rind of the fruit working backward,
encasing the seed. Mute button for shame
between mammals. Color of jade and of moss.
Thank you intimacy with the highways
and burrow-holes inside her body. You,
ambassador of our afternoons, bridging me
to the most unnamable part of my most
unwavering friend. She is boxy and pelted,
celebrates me without speaking,
is one thousand paws pressed to the tip
of my nose. She doesn't wear clothes.
And from you I have learned to lean down
toward the ground where she tells her true
stories. She's a funnel of lava, fleeced sacrum
of earth and affection. Of course stars rush
right through her. Of course she evacuates
asteroids! And you are the hyphen between
her name and mine. Every day you umbilical cord
me to something other than keyboard, other
than inbox. Lay even the edge of my hand
into the grass, onto the autumn, engine my feet
to the sidewalk, to the sirens and the place
beyond sirens. Yes, you've stunk up my house

with your imperfect membrane. Have betrayed me,
split stocking or knifed gut of a mackerel. But how
you have whispered your plastic Parseltongue
language into my sleepwalking devotion. Been
wedding canopy, saxophone song, officiant
of our daily marriage. Every walk is a gift,
every time I forget you at home, let
my dog leave her name scrawled hot
and brown on the sidewalk. I think
I'm supposed to feel bad, but I feel like,
lucky sidewalk, for knowing a love
so sprawling and wet as I know it.

THE OLDEST FORM OF PRAYER

Who do you think invented the first instrument? you ask me, each eye opening an aperture with the curving, softest blade into my eyes.

You are obsessed with outer space and also with the brain. Your spiraled science reveals no edges, more darkness velvet and praiseful expanding from the bright seed at its center.

This is a love song. Symphonic and silent as the drone of the cosmos, and loud as the brain is long, when stretched across a lab table.

This is a love song the way the brain is a humming organ. Not unlike the boiler in a basement giving off its whirring and its heat. Love hums like the boiler and whirs like the boiler. Cells synapse, heat in the brain, love's industrious labor.

In my worship I'll climb to the outer deck of a spacecraft and declare you. Like crying you out from the rooftops, except for the swallowing silence and the burning of stars.

You, all eyelashes, squared hips, and hands. *What is the most dangerous thing that happens in outer space?*

The first instrument was a flute. A reed, or cleaved from lightweight wood, or hewn from the bone of a mammal no longer running and already singing in the hands of its crafter as they carved it.

The ancient form of the love song, its date and origin widely contested. Some composers wander the gardens while others become night sky explorers.

When you leave me you will become a current of wind riding the cloudy stain of a galaxy.

The strangest form of science is music, or the way we notate devotion with symbols and numbers.

Entire days spent circling the small mound of soft flesh at the center of your palm, its callused pink moat. Lover as universe. The connective tissue of blackness and asteroids that floats between planets. Lover as the sinews of nothingness that fasten planet to planet.

Did you know that the bodies of astronauts stretch in outer space? How after spending six months in the absence of gravity, the body of a space traveler will expand and relax, up to three percent taller.

Without coercion, just the body uncompelled toward the center. The earth too far to be remembered. Brain enveloped in the absence of light. The possibility of becoming larger.

The first love song was rocket. The first rocket was touch. The first touch was the last touch. The last touch was remembered, carried by neurons and stars. It seems that the brain, when confronted by infinite darkness, can become itself.

NOW WE LIVE TOGETHER

My lover is eating a popsicle
and kisses me at the cold center
of lips teeth purple it is
sloppier wetter softer more
joyful than you can imagine.

Writing about happiness
is so boring.

It involves waking first beside them
and closing the bedroom door
as I tuck myself against lavender
morning in the kitchen.
Later when they wake up
their hand grazes my hip. They sit
down to practice their breath
while I leave for work.

It involves large pots of soup
they simmer for me full of cabbage.
One cabbage can yield a surprising
quantity of soup, so we knife it apart
and delight at its ruffled density.
The cut open crossfolds
look like outlines of bodies
with v's nested between legs.

We tell jokes about our ancestors
passing one another in the aisles of trains
riding between Belarus, Transylvania.
The jokes are funny until they're not
funny, since trains aren't neutral

and people like us who have sex
with these bodies aren't supposed to be
making a home.

We ask our ancestors with their secrets
and with their train tickets
and grocery lists for their blessings
and then we go for a walk
on the beach wearing jackets.
When my lover trips in the sand
I'm down there beside them
and they say, *thank you for falling
with me*.

Writing about happiness
isn't exactly a love letter
to my great grandmother
but it isn't *not* that either;
her husband died when she
was younger than I am,
she never remarried.

BECAUSE IT IS ELUL

I drove two long silent hours to get here,
cut through an August green as lust
and as my body falls, at last, into the sea—

tumulting, crashing all about me—
the skinny man a few yards off shouts
careful! crooks his wire finger toward

the breakers, warning: *sting rays*.
Water bats. Winged frisbees fan
through salted chaos, their shapes slice

the cresting waves. Shadows moving
behind stained glass, dusky diamonds
fluent in the ebb and swag of ocean

roaring ocean, salivating sea, I stagger out
from the cliff of backward blue, my breath
floats before me like a bell.

All afternoon they come, a moving clot,
dark ribbon dragging through the water.
Waterborn pilots parading their shark skin

and cartilage vessels, tucking and soaring
and migrating somewhere.
I sit and watch, spotlit

in the hot mind of August,
lucky, lucky victim
of this grandeur.

I came to drop my hands into the sand,
to name each regret, each evidence of all
that's cracked in me like sun-starched

seaweed before the burling waves.
The King is in the dunes, my knees
are gnashed into the grains.

This time each year, we throw things
into the water. Bread crumbs carrying
our failures, our bright faults.

But watching those swarthy ghost fish, each one
big as a window reflecting the sun off the side
of my car, I don't want to throw anything in.

I want to be whole, I say aloud to the sea,
*I want you to be whole. I want the nightmare
of our separation to end.*

The wave crests, the travelers revealed
again and again. This is the story God tells

in a language I no longer speak.

WHEN MY SISTER VISITS

a cup of milk within the saucer of her mouth,
incisors coffee-stained and pearled. She tips
her frothy tongue into my morning cup, it swirls.
I don't understand her, but I do trust she won't
drug me. Sister, moonstone, ratchet, strobe.
I try to dress for work. She grabs the other sock,
garbles the zipper with her knuckle. I step into
the jumpsuit of her voice, my arms distend
the sleeves. She drapes me: humid, green, and
photosynthesizing. She drapes me, so I stay.

WE THANKED HER BY DIGGING A HOLE

It is how we say thanks.

The hole had four corners and its walls
were built of earth-psalm, thirsting.

Her sister and her lover dragged out
two boxes of books by the hole

and the rabbi told us, *reach in,*
pull out a book. The books smelled

sour on their yellowed pages but the unbled
words told oldest stories, carried prayers

penciled over by centuries of fathers
inked by excrement of beetles

and the feather of a scribe.
First we lowered her body

into a box, then the box
into a hole, and then

the books.
We had to drop them in, and listen

to them thunk against the box,
against the soil, echo of earth

where libraries have been harvested,
grains of sand becoming paper

now a small collection of everything
being returned. We lined the hole with books

until we could not see the box
or the body laid within it. I stood

at the edge of the place where books go to die
to mingle with the great mouth

that unthreads their bindings with its tongue.
We call it *geniza* and we will call it *grave*

and it will unbind her and she'll turn
to the page of the book in the place

beyond the place where light touches,
there among mysteries throbbingly quiet

her mind blooming a great field of language,
her retinas decaying, forever opened, her eyes.

FRAGMENTS OF AN ANTHEM

In our generation nobody doesn't talk
about the melting,

nobody doesn't talk about the throbbing,
nobody doesn't throb about the typing.

When we are born we know about
the screaming trees. We see their

symphonies flicker the dark eyes
of our mothers, we throb about

the mothers, we type
about the fires.

When we are born we know the milk
is curdled water, but we drink it,

we are grateful, and we pray.
In our generation prayer sounds

like limbs in sand on coastlines, rivers,
sidewalks, gilded pools of puddled rain.

Prayer sounds like sweat and sex
and sadness. Prayer, the gratitude the earth gave

back to us in exchange for the death
of our species. Sometimes it sounds

like we are yelling but in fact
we are praying.

Oh, how we pray,
snap our hips, limp our wrists,

and Oh, how we long for prostrations.
We cook what is dead and we eat it.

Nobody doesn't grieve when they dance,
no body is not an elegy body—

the ankles, the floodlights, the whimpering
shoulders, the fleshdance of chance

and decay. Fleshgreiving, bloodsongs,
Oh, how we want, how we are each other's

blood, how we pain this, we learn every time.
Learn again that we are each other's blood

but not flesh. In our generation
nobody doesn't talk about flesh—

how it burns, how we burn for it,
how before us generations burnt

villages, continents, burnt aquifers, grave sites
naming the flesh, in the names of the flesh.

When we are born we know that someone came
before us, someone cut their teeth before us here

on this roiling century. We are throbbed
by forests, flickered by mothers,

we ache and we dance and we try and we pray.
In our generation we hold each other

by the hip, we hold each other
by the dusty moonlight,

we hold each other
by the chin.

I can't sleep on spring mornings because the birds
plunge their throats into my mind and pull me up
toward the breaking of day. If I thought I was alone
I'd never get out of bed, but I do get out, take the pill,
shuffle around. Everything whispers an origin
story. A clay mug that has been crust of earth.
Coffee grounds that have been crust of earth.
Psychopharmaceuticals composed of earth, salt.
In the back of the house a large plastic bag contains
all the other plastic bags, like an unbreathing creature
carrying our sins tattooed to her handles. She too
has been petroleum, hydrocarbon, rock strata, resin.
Intricate odorless ribbons of plastic. What is the name
for an object composed of smaller composites of itself?
On spring mornings I blink through the window and check
on the garden. Chew marks where the urban squirrel
has announced his mouth to the kale. We had to bring in
the potted sage yesterday after he so thoroughly ransacked it.
He lives inside our front awning, gnawed through the string lights
I wove over the house beams. Neighboring him, a family of wrens
or finches perhaps. The straw of their nest pokes like a cowlick
from the seams between wood panels just over the door. They
moved in a week after we did, and we laugh, we call them
our tenants. We put a mezuzah there, hand-penned scroll
with the name of God inked onto parchment. The ink
is crushed insect excrement, gall nuts, logwood, and soot.
Copper and sulfate burned through a smoothed hide of goat.
Every plunder a prayer. This spring a bell rung with quiet.
We haven't had a friend, a child, or a plumber into our home
for three months. We circle the block, press longing against keys
wired plastic in motherboards. It's Mother's Day, we pull up her face
on the screen. Her teeth flash out over cobalt and iron. We say mother
and beneath it our breath makes tiny gasps—magnesium, aluminum,

morning. *Mother* a thing composed of smaller composites. A house is.
A garden. On spring mornings I play my part in the kaleidoscope
of planet, pandemic. I worship the earth and I ravage her, pour
out my coffee grinds into the raised beds and *alone* is a word
more hollow than sickness. Sickness knits me to beetles, it weaves
me to wood, it shows me the mirror in which my creature face
greets me. When the marigold seeds don't come up, I lay a stone
on the soil. When the chives crowd one another and their hairs start
to brown, I call my mom. She says: *you thought they were your tenants,
just like I did when you lived inside me.* But there was an ocean
boiling that great house into birth.

You don't know where they came from only that they're here now, and the email from the arborist says *kill kill kill* and their outer bodies are slate machinery gray but when you smash them between two chips of tree bark or clomp into them with your boots, a sudden eruption of lantern red, the inner lining of those curtainy wings, that red at once triumphant and subtle, for which they are named Spotted Lantern Flies, enemy of all maples, gorgers of sap with mouths like a straw, *we don't know how to be rid of them*, the arborist tells us, so we must try everything: observe, scrape eggs, share news with your neighbors, he says *I'm taking down hundreds a day*, and that sickening satisfaction in killing them off, because it is so rare to go to war with a slow-moving bug, large as a thumb and arriving by thousands to our already scanty-treed city, sitting there on the trunk laying eggs over unhurried days, too easy to scoop up and flatten, yet always more of them swarming this town and its figs and its willows, and word gets around that we're being invaded, lectures and flyers at the public library branch, neighbors lending one another their ladders, and you're wondering, is it our fierce love of trees, is it our futuristic belief that the green lungs of this city will feed us, is it a middle-class defense of neighborhood beauty, is it the nagging desire we have for an enemy, is it our envy for the Spotted Lantern Fly invasive and thriving at a time when it seems our own species blights our own survival on this plump spinning garden, we know they're invasive because they come from some other country, sounds like *not in my backyard*, sounds like *go back where you came from*, and we know we want to be rid of them because trees are what breathes us, we know it's unnatural to live in a place made of concrete and steel, so we defend its soil and its canopies, more than we ever defend one another, more feverishly than we will remember to honor our transience, to honor the need for swarm and survival, we say *keep them out, keep our trees safe*, sounds like *keep them from our children, our front yards, and our women*, you leave town for a weekend and when you come back there are two perched on the maple outside your house, huddled together, touching wings tucked against little mechanical bodies, the leaves of the maple growing a fiery red in the late light of October and they're higher up on the tree than you can reach with your arms so you leave them, wonder when you'll get to them later, if you'll get to them later, what to do, what should you do, about the way people can't tell nature and concrete, human and insect, migrant and invader, honor and greed, violence and benevolence, summer and autumn, neighbor and neighbor apart.

A POEM ABOUT A BOOK ABOUT VENEZUELA

Did the Psalmist feel done at the end
of his litany? Shaking and sweating
and words chipping off him?

Bruise-tremor of language—
a book of lush silences
inhaled, held breath

between title and end page,
a phantom twin book
standing just to the left,

breathing its book breaths full of words I can sense
but can't read, I don't mean Spanish or English.
In this way too it is Bible, a book crowded

by words that aren't actually
in it, in this way too it is codex
of love or survival.

By the book, meaning: there are rules to this.

Book about mountains, book about zinc,
book about grandeur, book about grief,
book of stories other people tell about book,

of words scrawled around book.
Book of leaving, arriving,
book about shades of green,

textbook of bird beaks,
album of economics.

Book of silt,
book of drowning,
book with multiple nations living inside.

Ghost book, book of souls,
book of soil, not maps.

Bookish, meaning: with or without other people.

Velvet leaves, binding loose,
labels unstuck from bottles.

Demonstration flyers
smothered
in petrol, lit to burn.

Book volcanic with glass
or aluminum, pressed into mirrors

not topographic or diagrammatic,
not a book containing
the right names for card games.

Book-ended: you have a beginning and you have a conclusion.

Coda of night sounds, thickening
night streets in hot cities, index of stars.

Unalphabetical, not
genealogical,

and *yes*, book of revolutionary
figures cramming the spine.

How many immigrants does it take
to fasten a book, how many fingers bandage
its paper together, how many mouths press

the stitching, write it on air, audio recorded
in how many languages?
And where will the electricity

come from to power up the machine,
where will the microphone come from
when the oil runs out?

Back into the boat, bent pages, wet float.

Somewhere history-succulent, book
dripping with loss, pages droning
with question, illegible answers.

The *Good Book*: the great hulking mountain
from which book was born.

SLEEPING IN HURRICANE SEASON

I remember other beds in other places.
Luster of cicadas. Night street lined with jade.

Summer of desperate, pounding water. We sleep
with our heads hovering over the alley.

The book I'm reading is supposedly
about whiteness. The author

spends her pages confessing
the many people she's ignored.

I want to say that without its fricative
edge, but I am learning to become more brittle,

not less. Islands of the Caribbean stripped
to their lowest layers of soil, of thirst.

I live now in a flat place and sleep without incline.
Night rolls fitful around us, untucks our blanket.

I haven't learned that unfricative language,
but I imagine it like a night without air

conditioning units. A softness embedding
the air. Night turns now to that meshy net

of September. In September I always learn
something new. Still, it is called a Tropical Storm.

Dreams of water-choked houseboats, sog-bent
bodies of trees. My fist curls in the night.

An island is a bruise in a flesh-world
of water. A bead embedded in the promise

of its own demise. When I read the book
about whiteness I think of people out there

floating around. Surrounded by something they love
that will kill them. Silence in the night is heavy

like water. We float in it like water.
It gives us our lives.

EMBLANQUECER

Prompt: put your contradicting parts in dialogue
with one another. What can dialogue be
if some tongues are composed of iron or blade?
How does tenderness speak to brutality?
Does brutality wave a national flag?
Say cloaks traded for jackets,
throats traded for jackals.
Say fringes on garments became cold clutch of pearls.
Say the promise of steel made of paper and blood,
say promise and mean what a promise is always:
no more dying, no more dead, no more dying.
A people with an anthem meant to beat out
the drone, to out-fox the angel of death and his armies
of rapists and gluttons, say who wouldn't run
from that army? But running is different
than dancing and jackals don't look right
in jackets. Ask what we gambled
in order to thrive off the fingers
of children we claimed were not
our own children, ask what
does it mean if you can live
in a city for decades
without riding
the bus?

GHAZAL FOR A YEAR

That year we learned to bend our knees, to stretch our palms
flat on the ground, attention grew a garden of our eyes.

We remembered pencils, hand-washed dishes, started sleeping
more. Stole time from empire's cabinets, packed time into our eyes.

We said *I don't know* more often to more people. Remembered
humming trees, how generous the sky, we stopped trying to look

cool while dancing. Remembered bodies without war against
the asphalt: shoulder tips, finger bones, clear palliated eyes.

Our thousand heels sang patience. Or: our thousand heels sang rage.
Remembered death, laid stones down there. Tribute to lost eyes.

Remembered how to boil stock from scrap. Ground rushed to meet us
as we fell, every feeling came to flood us, every ancestor's worn eyes.

We bowed our heads, our hair fell out, grief came over us, a starshower
to brighten and to wreck, to level us, and open, finally, our eyes.

HALLELUYAH

I'm a molar wedged deep inside   the back of her mouth. Oh,
the way she runs her tongue   over me feels for scraps but
I feel gathered in. Oh, the way   she says my name, everything
crowded into it, how fully she   turns me, inside-out like a garment
shakes the sand out of me.   How she knows and unknows me
pushes me away and is cosmos,   the burning nose of each star.
I'm a seed, she's soil folding me in.   Compost of phone lines, trash bins
beers drunk on rooftops in cities. She   is crooning and rageful, sweaters
and droughts, she does not speak   but Oh, how she speaks
the sun woven through tree   limbs, her voice in the oceanic lifting
of humans in song. Her voice   roasts salt into zucchini, electrifies
hungering limbs of entangled   teenagers, lays palms against
every war zone, collision, every   waterlogged island, her voice
every mouth of every bird   and every volume of Talmud. *Oh child*
she shovels light into me,   *Oh child*, she taught me to hold a body
with my own hands while all   the breath left it, *Oh small thing*
she carves her voice through   my mind, *small small cherished thing*
her voice mountains into me,   hurricanes into me, crashes
around me and the gratitude hurts   so much I think it will rip me clean
end to end. She wraps me in worry,   swaddles me against city, she teaches
me love so I'll always be hungry.   She teaches me Hebrew so I'll always
be longing, so I can use the language   of my greatest great uncles to thank her
to say please, all of our eyes wilting into   the mystery, the words crack like frozen
rain on our eyelashes, shake all   of our heads. *Oh vessel*, she whispers
as I mourn and surrender, *Oh precious*   *you're so important and unimportant*
you're so good and already forgotten.   She says, *Stop hurting yourself, stop*
hurting others. I'm on my knees,   she is that burning in my bent
is the night, cloaks me   when I can't sleep, *Take a walk, touch*
all of my quilts, says, *Bang*   *any object against another to find me.*

WE WALKED DAHLIAS TO HER FRONT PORCH

In the darkness of her labor, didn't know
if they would help. Hairy pink

and orange faces laughing
into ours. All night I marveled

at her distance. A cave
of pain and possibility. Not alone, but

alone of me. Carnage and topographies
she'll never un-travel now.

Another autumn, another poem
about babies. Babies tumbling over us

raining into us, hard-won and brute
with wisdom. In the morning I wait

heart jerking for a photograph
anticipating doughy knuckles, crumpled

eyelids weathered like an after-storm
of petals. Every hour it doesn't come

my inbox is another landscape lengthening
between us. What have they said already

to one another? Hard latch, receding
organs. Songs I will not learn to sing.

A bruise is blooming
over me, becoming me.

I THOUGHT I WAS DONE WRITING ABOUT MY DEAD

but they surface in me, still.
Tonight a memory of him

on top of a mountain crowned
in autumn, him extending

his long knobby arm
and at the end of it, a thumb.

His callused, bobbing thumb
balanced at the tip of that

arm, his eyes glassless,
purposeful, honing

on the thumb. Swinging his arm
from side to side and locking

his retinal optic nerves only
on that thumb, a valley

of browns and velvet reds
sprawling out of focus behind

the anchoring appendage.
His knees bent slightly,

shoulders crisp against
the season's breath, he almost

could have taken flight off
that bald-faced mountaintop

if not for the thumb
that held him like a dark

spool of thread
attached to earth.

I thought I had recorded
every single memory of him

but that's not the way it works—
our dead coming up for air in us

as if they were the muscled
backs of whales, a memory

cutting upward through the break
in a wave of the waking world,

a long thick drink of oxygen.
On the mountain

he was showing me exercises
from the vision improvement

course he'd been taking, his eyes
bolted onto the farthest bud

of his own distant limb,
the whole world streaming

just beyond his sight in a slurried
fog of movement.

He said he thought his eyes
were getting stronger. And isn't it

always the dead suggesting to us
the possibility of the impossible?

Not what's beyond our sight, but
what is there, contained within it.

GHAZAL FOR GOD & WELLBUTRIN

Took me years to learn touch is done with hands,
song is what the throat does, how to see with eyes.

Before: mind popping rocks, soupy melody, brain cradle
days of fur pulled over thinking place, feeling fog be eyes.

Sand abrading ridges cracked between ceramic—gyri, sulci
hosting hardness, sorrow telling me I shouldn't be, bleeds eyes.

I remember when J was still alive. Laughing with him about madness
he said "I like you so much, maybe I should take it too"—reprise.

Then the first time I discovered Boredom, that blank blessing. What
is time without hateful voices clamoring inside? Started to realize.

Now my hand is lodestone in the mornings, draws open glowing bottle, pill
like pit of stone fruit in my palm. Got healthcare but it isn't free, prize.

Not yet awake, small ritual of lips takes shape, *Blessed are You, One
who makes me in Your image, by Your will*, invoke a day of seen I's.

Thank you releasing agent, reuptake inhibitor, converted metabolite, thank
you white noise, pink liver, thank you pink brain, green skin, green eyes.

Blessed is the One who made me incomplete, say: *Broken*, say: *One who
fashioned world of ragged siblings, jagged verges, nowhere to flee eyes.*

Tongue presses pill down into muscled throat, say: *Holy, Blessed*, blinking
sleep away and sadness. Trying every day to see me, see me, see, devise.

Blessed is the One who also cannot heal Herself without the help of chemists,
novelists, and farmers, pharmacologists. She, crowned with demons, doesn't demonize.

THE POET CONSIDERS IF HER BODY BELONGS TO HER

In the mirror some edges taper off
into light, light-filled sound. Here

are great waves of breath riding into
and leaving the body. Doors spin

on their built-in revolvers, the opens
and shuts of you. Take a breath.

Everyone cycles through.
Mostly the body is exits, arrivals.

Mostly on-ramps, back doors, trap
doors, fire escapes. Red carpets

rolled out on sternum and tongue.
Mostly mailboxes, runways, trade port

and train station. Skin cells stacking
for decades like bricks into doorways

and archways, gateways and courtyards.
The body may be less like a house

and more like an airport—
organ of transit, fluorescent

at dawn. An airport, no matter
the hour, is a churning.

In the mirror breath stills the filled body
but it is not only breath that enters

and leaves. It is dust, streetlights,
and rages. Secrets and weather. Voices

of metal and earth, other names, other people
altogether, arrive and depart, land and take off.

How many brutal and generous citizens,
tourists of the body, built this coming

and going thing of clutter and silence—
every scrap, every linoleum tile

belonging to all of its architects, all
of its authors. How many travelers,

cellists sliding wheeled
instruments down lit corridors,

belonging to no one
or everyone, belonging to

anyone who has laid a hand
at her edge.

WHEN MY SISTER VISITS

she holds a mirror to my face, smudged
from some soil-drenched mountain, clumps
gumming the palms of her hands. *Look*, she says,
look at yourself. I see overgrown tennis courts,
spindle-shanked trees, and the sidewalk in front
of my abuela's house cracked and raised by octopus vines.
My sister enrolls me in a beauty pageant and each competitor
has a parking lot instead of a face. Littered with rain,
wet leaves suctioned to pavement and foreheads
of cars. Their skin hot amber and coal.
I see the exhaust fumes of airports.
Look again, she says, lifting the mirror.

The day after is Halloween, the neighborhood jeweled, dazzling with transformers and zombie ballerinas. The entire neighborhood pours into and out of itself like two glasses of water. Washes through its own ache like soap suds and buckets of rain. Pumps itself through a sieve. You've never seen such a movement of bodies, the sidewalk an ant colony of incredible hulks, werewolves wheeling small circles, the streets tinsel with motion like schools of fish. In this sudden secular ritual you watch, give away, review tonight's nouns: *trick*, *thanks*, gesture toward *repair*, which is not *reparation*. Strangers pass so many sugar-encased objects between outstretched hands. And there is some flavor of healing in all of this laughter blistering through all of this pain. Black neighbors and white neighbors exchange the smallest unit of interconnection. A Tootsie Roll here, three bags of Hershey bars later. The neighborhood pretends it's composed of love and equal distribution. And you, white Jewish latina perched in a tree beside the condemned lantern fly, cousins of the first generation, occupying the block. Titter how it titters, monitor all those flying wrists, flickering palms in the street. Arco de iris broken apart, splinters into plastic jack-o'-lanterns clutched from the bottom. Sacred celebration of none of your countries except your most country. You didn't realize how much witches were still in fashion. And it does feel like love out on the streets: this is a festival, this is how a festival feels in a city of desire and ruin, of birth and of murder, of cops and of children. Even on the block where it happened—kids, parents in costumes. Everyone involved in the possibility of what else we could be.

LOVE LETTER

—for Bibi

You are going to die. Soon.

With you go all the pine trees in Romania, all the pine needles,
all the needletop rooftops of the already bulldozed villages. With you

goes your brother's childhood nickname a thousand trampled
flowers your shaking hand against my smaller hand that sharpest

shade of blue at Puerto Azul that humming space between the first
language you learned and the second, the eighth language.

What I first wanted to say was, I don't think I'm going to
have a child. And with that unhad child goes your wooden ruler

sewing scissors the E at the beginning of your name,
which is a name I would have honored—unhooking

its first letter, dignified and simple, and affixing it to that child's
name. Today is the day after your one hundred and first

birthday. Stained glass for eyes, sequined web of hair.
I want to tell you I have named that unhad child, have held

their little map hand, all the veins encoded there. What do you
call the top part of a hand? Not the palm. The bone-protruding

side, at least for all the women in our family. What do you call
a hand with highways on it, hand patched from passports

bribed or stolen? Here's what I think I'm trying to say:
somewhere in a field of wildflowers unthreatened

by the rising heat and melting sun, you and I sit together
on a log. I say, *I love you.* And, *I'm not having a child.*

You put your hand on mine.

Acknowledgments

Grateful acknowledgment to the editors and staff of the following journals where these poems first appeared, sometimes under different titles and in earlier forms:

Adroit Journal: "Self-Portrait with Airplane Turbulence"

Black Warrior Review: "Ghazal for God & Wellbutrin"

Boiler Journal: "Halleluyah"

Canthius: "Here" (p. 54), "A Poem About a Book About Venezuela"

COMP: An Interdisciplinary Journal: "Abecedario," "Emblanquecer" (p. 61), "Ghazal for a First Lover," "Ghazal for a Year"

Fearsome Critters: A Millennial Arts Journal: "Now We Live Together"

Foglifter Journal: "Banishing Loneliness," "God Queers the Mountain," "Imaginative Exercise in the Study of Epigenetics," "It Isn't Easy To Speak"

Frontier Poetry: "Here" (p. 14)

Gigantic Sequins: "The Oldest Form of Prayer"

Hold: A Journal: "After Pulse"

Interim: "Fragments of an Anthem," "I Thought I Was Done Writing About My Dead"

Iowa Review: "Sleeping in Hurricane Season"

The Journal: "Family Is an Illumination of Shoulders"

Minola Review: "A Poem with Two Memories of Venezuela"

Ninth Letter: "When My Sister Visits"

Pedestal Magazine: "We Thanked Her by Digging a Hole"

Plenitude Magazine: "Theology"

Rabbit: A Journal for Nonfiction Poetry: "Might Kindred"

So to Speak Journal: "Emblanquecer" (p. 3)

Southern Indiana Review (Ruth Awad Poetry Pick): "Immigrant Elegy for Ávila"

Third Coast: "Love Letter," "The Poet Considers If Her Body Belongs To Her," "Prologue"

Tinderbox Journal: "Dendrochronology of Hair," "Letter to Myself from My Great Grandmother"

Waxwing: "Falling Out"

West Trestle Review: "Here" (p. 74)

"A Poem with Two Memories of Venezuela" won the 2020 Minola Review Poetry Contest, judged by Doyali Islam, and was anthologized in *The Best Small Fictions* (Sonder Press, 2021).

"The Synagogue Membership Assembles to Discuss the Fascist Presidency" was published in Linke Fligl's *Ushpi(zine): A Sukkot Zine & DIY Ritual Guide, Ki Li Ha'aretz, Vol. 1*.

"Ghazal for God & Wellbutrin" was republished in *Verse Daily*.

Thank you friends, community, neighbors, and mentors. This book is animated by your voices, your stories, and your light. To be loved, guided, challenged, and held by you is what gives me the strength to write anything at all. This life with you is a wonder.

Overflowing gratitude to the teams at *Prairie Schooner* and the University of Nebraska Press for the time and care it took to usher this book so generously into the world. Thank you to Aimee Nezhukumatathil, Hilda Raz, and Kwame Dawes, the final judges of the 2021 Raz/Shumaker Prairie Schooner Book Prize in Poetry, for this incredible opportunity. Thank you to Rithika Merchant for your mesmerizing cover art. Huge thanks to Nicole Sealey and Shira Erlichman for the blessing of your reading. And especially, deep gratitude to Kwame Dawes for the honor of working with you as my editor. I am forever indebted to all of you for believing in these poems.

An ocean of thanks to my writing siblings, who have been early readers of nearly every poem in this book and whose kinship in the world of words is a daily source of generosity, trust, and tenderness: Rage Hezekiah, Tessa Micaela, MJ Kaufman, Olga Dugan, Talia Young, Sukriti Nayar, Sarah Levy, mai c. doan, Avra Shapiro, and Sarah O'Neal. Thank you to Aurora Levins-Morales for being the poet-liturgist of my heart and an always role model. A deep bow to everyone who has taught me poetry, especially Jill Magi, Jen Hofer, Rick Benjamin, Jay Deshpande, Shira Erlichman, and Jon Sands. Thank you for creating sacred spaces of learning and growth for these poems and for me. A rocket ship of gratitude to Jon and all the Emotional Historians—the luck I feel to be in poetry community with you is boundless. Finally, bottomless wells of gratitude to Sasha Warner-Berry for always getting my books over the finishing line with your fierce wisdom and friendship.

To my spiritual communities, Kol Tzedek and SVARA, thank you for being a home where the heart can both grow and rest, and for the foundation of kindness, courage, resilience, and spirit we've created together.

Gracias Alicia Rusoja y Joha Mateo Van Osten for being my compas in the distance and intimacy of Venezuela.

To my parents, Dina and Pablo, and to my brother, Daniel, for traveling this life with me, for permitting me to write about our world and our lineage, and for the abundant, loving ways you hold me. To Hodi, for filling these pages with your big eyes and furry heart.

And to Jess, for a love that makes every day and every word possible. For every dance in the kitchen and every quiet morning where this work can take shape. What grace to make art, family, and life with you.

To my ancestors, and to my beloved dead, with whom these poems emerged collaboratively. Especially to Jonah, for all that you continue to bless my life with. And my Bibi Elly, mi única, mi corazon.

Thank you, Hashem, fountain of all poems, for everything.

And to you, reader, for the blessing of your time and your presence. I can't say thank you enough.

Notes

EPIGRAPHS

The opening epigraphs of this book are from Ursula K. Le Guin's *The Wave in the Mind: Talks and Essays on the Writer, the Reader, and the Imagination* and Franny Choi's video-poem in the Queer Check-Ins series on the Smithsonian Asian Pacific American Center website.

SELF-PORTRAIT WITH AIRPLANE TURBULENCE

This poem's final stanza refers to tahara, the Jewish practice of ritually bathing the dead before burial.

THEOLOGY

"They taught me every Thou is a funnel for the big bright You" refers to Martin Buber's theological work *I and Thou*.

The line "put your queer shoulder to the wheel" borrows from Allen Ginsberg's "America."

"Selah" and "Hoshana" are exclamations of exaltation and petition, found in the Tanakh/Hebrew Bible. "Apa" means "father" in Hungarian and is the word we use for grandfathers in my family.

EMBLANQUECER

In Spanish, "emblanquecer," which appears as the title of two poems in this collection, means "to whiten." It refers to the specific "whitening the race" campaigns in Latin America that promoted European immigration and access to social and economic privilege for European immigrants. Here it is also used to refer to the assimilation of some Latinx and Jewish people into whiteness and white supremacy culture in the United States.

IMMIGRANT ELEGY FOR ÁVILA

This poem remembers the drive from Simón Bolívar International Airport to my grandmother's house in Caracas, which winds through the mountain El Ávila, known as "el pulmón de la ciudad," the lungs of the city.

GHAZAL FOR A FIRST LOVER

The three ghazals in this book are written with gratitude for this Arabic poetic form of Persian origin.

GOD QUEERS THE MOUNTAIN

The story referred to and reimagined in this poem comes from the Babylonian Talmud, Shabbat 88a, in which God lifts Mount Sinai over the Israelite people, threatening them to accept Torah or be buried beneath the mountain.

AFTER PULSE

In memory of the forty-nine victims of the 2016 Pulse nightclub shooting in Orlando, Florida, over 90 percent of whom were Latinx queer people. Images and phrases in this poem were gathered from attending a Muslim, Jewish, and Christian vigil to honor the dead.

ODE TO THE POOP BAG

With thanks to Nava EtShalom for her line "the stars rush through you" from her poem "Recovery."

BECAUSE IT IS ELUL

Elul is the last Hebrew month before the new year begins, a period of intensive introspection and reconciliation. Jewish tradition teaches that in Elul, "the King is in the field," meaning that the divine is an intimate witness to our self-examination. In the new year a ritual called Tashlich is performed, where breadcrumbs are thrown into a body of water as a way of casting off one's failures and transgressions.

WE THANKED HER BY DIGGING A HOLE

In memory of Marlyn Grossman, z"l.

BANISHING LONELINESS

A mezuzah is a ritual object placed on the doorposts of Jewish homes, containing a roll of parchment with Hebrew verses of Torah scribed onto it.

I THOUGHT I WAS DONE WRITING ABOUT MY DEAD

In memory of Jonah Meadows Adels, z"l.

LOVE LETTER

For my grandmother Elena Rath de Goldstein, z"l.

In the Raz/Shumaker Prairie Schooner Book Prize in Poetry series

Cortney Davis, *Leopold's Maneuvers*

Rynn Williams, *Adonis Garage*

Kathleen Flenniken, *Famous*

Paul Guest, *Notes for My Body Double*

Mari L'Esperance, *The Darkened Temple*

Kara Candito, *Taste of Cherry*

Shane Book, *Ceiling of Sticks*

James Crews, *The Book of What Stays*

Susan Blackwell Ramsey, *A Mind Like This*

Orlando Ricardo Menes, *Fetish: Poems*

R. A. Villanueva, *Reliquaria*

Jennifer Perrine, *No Confession, No Mass*

Safiya Sinclair, *Cannibal*

Susan Gubernat, *The Zoo at Night*

Luisa Muradyan, *American Radiance*

Aria Aber, *Hard Damage*

Jihyun Yun, *Some Are Always Hungry*

Susan Nguyen, *Dear Diaspora*

Mónica Gomery, *Might Kindred*

To order or obtain more information on these or other University of Nebraska Press titles, visit nebraskapress.unl.edu.

Printed in the USA
CPSIA information can be obtained
at www.ICGtesting.com
CBHW031416210524
8886CB00003B/190